MORGAN HARPER NICHOLS

SUZANNE STABILE, SERIES EDITOR

FORTY DAYS ON
BEING A FIVE

ENNEAGRAM DAILY REFLECTIONS

An imprint of InterVarsity Press
Downers Grove, Illinois

InterVarsity Press
P.O. Box 1400, Downers Grove, IL 60515-1426
ivpress.com
email@ivpress.com

InterVarsity Press® is the book-publishing division of InterVarsity Christian Fellowship/USA®, a
movement of students and faculty active on campus at hundreds of universities, colleges, and schools
of nursing in the United States of America, and a member movement of the International Fellowship
of Evangelical Students. For information about local and regional activities, visit intervarsity.org.

All Scripture quotations, unless otherwise indicated, are taken from The Holy Bible, New
International Version®, NIV®. Copyright © 1973, 1978, 1984, 2011 by Biblica, Inc.™ Used by
permission of Zondervan. All rights reserved worldwide. www.zondervan.com. The "NIV" and "NIV
International Version" are trademarks registered in the United States Patent and Trademark Office by
Biblica, Inc.™

While any stories in this book are true, some names and identifying information may have been
changed to protect the privacy of individuals.

The publisher cannot verify the accuracy or functionality of website URLs used in this book beyond
the date of publication.

Enneagram figure by InterVarsity Press

All other figures are used courtesy of the author.

Cover design and image composite: David Fassett
Interior design: Daniel van Loon
Images: gold foil background: © Katsumi Murouchi / Moment Collection /
          Getty Images
       paper texture background: © Matthieu Tuffet / iStock / Getty Images Plus

ISBN 978-0-8308- 4750-1 (print)
ISBN 978-0-8308- 4751-8 (digital)

Printed in the United States of America ♾

Library of Congress Cataloging-in-Publication Data

Names: Nichols, Morgan Harper, 1990- author.
Title: Forty days on being a five / Morgan Harper Nichols.
Description: Downers Grove, Il : InterVarsity Press, [2021] | Series:
   Enneagram daily reflections
Identifiers: LCCN 2021012963 (print) | LCCN 2021012964 (ebook) | ISBN
   9780830847501 (print) | ISBN 9780830847518 (digital)
Subjects: LCSH: Personality—Religious aspects—Christianity—Meditations.
   | Enneagram.
Classification: LCC BV4597.57 .N53 2021 (print) | LCC BV4597.57 (ebook) |
   DDC 248.4—dc23
LC record available at https://lccn.loc.gov/2021012963
LC ebook record available at https://lccn.loc.gov/2021012964

| P | 20 | 19 | 18 | 17 | 16 | 15 | 14 | 13 | 12 | 11 | 10 | 9 | 8 | 7 | 6 | 5 | 4 | 3 | 2 |
| Y | 38 | 37 | 36 | 35 | 34 | 33 | 32 | 31 | 30 | 29 | 28 | 27 | 26 | 25 | 24 | 23 | 22 |

WELCOME TO
ENNEAGRAM DAILY REFLECTIONS

Suzanne Stabile

T he Enneagram is about nine ways of seeing. The reflections in this series are written from each of those nine ways of seeing. You have a rare opportunity, while reading and thinking about the experiences shared by each author, to expand your understanding of how they see themselves and how they experience others.

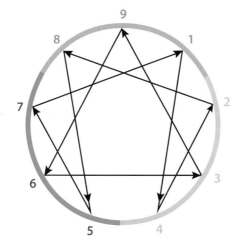

I've committed to teaching the Enneagram, in part, because I believe every person wants at least these two things: to belong, and to live a life that has meaning. And I'm sure that learning and working with the Enneagram has the potential to help all of us with both.

Belonging is complicated. We all want it, but few of us really understand it. The Enneagram identifies—with more accuracy than any other wisdom tool I know—why we can achieve belonging more easily with some people than with others. And it teaches us to find our place in situations and groups without having to displace someone else. (I'm actually convinced that it's the answer to world peace, but some have suggested that I could be exaggerating just a bit.)

If our lives are to have meaning beyond ourselves, we will have to develop the capacity to understand, value, and respect people who see the world differently than we do. We will have to learn to name our own gifts and identify our weaknesses, and the Enneagram reveals both at the same time.

The idea that we are all pretty much alike is shattered by the end of an introductory Enneagram workshop or after reading the last page of a good primer. But for those who are teachable and open to receiving Enneagram wisdom about each of the nine personality types, the shock is accompanied by a beautiful and unexpected gift: they find that they have more compassion for themselves and more grace for others and it's a guarantee.

The authors in this series, representing the nine Enneagram types, have used that compassion to move toward a greater understanding of themselves and others whose lives intersect with theirs in big and small ways. They write from experiences that reflect racial and cultural differences, and they have been influenced by their personal faith commitments. In working with spiritual directors, therapists, and pastors they identified many of their own habits and fears, behaviors and motivations, gifts and challenges. And they courageously talked with those who are close to them about how they are seen and experienced in relationship.

As you begin reading, I think it will be helpful for you to be generous with yourself. Reflect on your own life—where you've been and where you're going. And I hope you will consider the difference between change and transformation. *Change* is when we take on something new. *Transformation* occurs when something old falls away, usually beyond our control. When we see a movie, read a book, or perhaps hear a sermon that we believe "changed our lives," it will seldom, if ever, become transformative. It's a good thing and we may have learned a valuable life lesson, but that's not transformation. Transformation occurs when you have an experience that changes the way you understand life and its mysteries.

When my dad died, I immediately looked for the leather journal I had given to him years before with the request that he fill it with stories and things he wanted me to know. He had only written on one page:

Anything I have achieved or accomplished
in my life is because of the gift of your mother
as my wife. You should get to know her.

I thought I knew her, but I followed his advice, and it was one of the most transformative experiences of my life.

From a place of vulnerability and generosity, each author in this series invites us to walk with them for forty days on their journeys toward transformation. I hope you will not limit your reading to only your number. Read about your spouse or a friend. Consider reading about the type you suspect represents your parents or your siblings. You might even want to read about someone you have little affection for but are willing to try to understand.

You can never change *how* you see, but you can change what you *do* with how you see.

ON BEING A FIVE

For as long as I can remember, I have felt most comfortable as a wallflower. I enjoy being the observer leaning against the wall, taking everything in from afar. I have long had a natural inclination to retreat into my mind so that I might feel a little more capable and competent in the world. I felt different from others, especially when it came to social situations. As a result, I would compare myself to others and conclude that my way of being in the world was "wrong" and there was in fact something wrong with me.

When I discovered the Enneagram a few years ago, it felt like a map was unfolding. The Enneagram is an ancient tool that helps identify the specific ways we get lost or stuck across the landscape of life and also how we can find our way home, where we can become more and more of who we are meant to be. There are nine different personalities that illuminate different ways of being in the world, and I discovered that I was a Five. I was able to see things about myself that I had never had language for before. Suddenly, the path before me felt a little less lonely.

As a Five, I show up in the world as an observer. I live in pursuit of knowledge, seeking to learn and prepare myself to be capable and competent in the world. I desire to be useful; however, I tell myself that in order to do this, I must spend time away from others preparing to be in the world.

Seeing the Enneagram as a map was revelatory. Suddenly, I could see the various aspects of myself as a part of a greater landscape. On this map were many terrains—oceans, rivers, canyons, and valleys—and they all worked together. Yes, there were low places, but there were high places too. There were also a thousand places in between.

I discovered that the parts of myself I had previously seen as obstacles that kept me from being "normal" were actually ways I could grow. And not only grow in knowledge about what it meant to be a Five but grow closer to God. I could finally see that I didn't have to fix myself or have a certain personality that seemed acceptable in the world before I could breathe deep and surrender into grace that gives freedom to journey home—as a Five.

The basic desire of the Five is to be capable and competent. We seek to understand and we fear being helpless. We are driven by a pursuit of knowledge that can at times cause us to live in our heads. We find comfort in our safe places and reading nooks. We can spend a lot of our time thinking, contemplating, and searching for insight.

If this sounds like you or someone you know, I hope that this forty-day journey provides insight and encouragement on how to be present as a Five or with the Five in your life. Because many Fives tend to be a bit more reserved and private, connecting with a Five can be challenging. You may find yourself wanting closeness, but the Five you love doesn't seem to open up. I hope this daily journey provides a window into the soul of a Five—an individual who is deeply in tune, sensitive, and longing to connect in a unique way.

One of the beautiful things about the Enneagram is its diversity, and my journey is one of many ways that the various aspects of the Five are illuminated in the world.

I have written short prayers and reflections for the end of each reading. For some days there is only a prayer and for others only a reflection. Feel free to use them as starting points for your quiet devotional time, daily reflections, or conversations as you carry on your journey as a Five or as you go deeper with the Five in your life.

Along the way you will find a few readings labeled "an invitation." In these I shift from speaking of my own experience to speaking to you, the reader. So as we begin I want to offer the following invitation for Fives and everyone else.

On this lifelong journey of learning and growing, may we never forget our gifts. May we never forget that amid all of our fears of not having enough energy, of thinking we are helpless, of fearing we are incompetent, there is more beneath the surface. The waves of life may toss tirelessly against the boat, but beneath the deep blue there is stillness. There is peace. With a Five, there is always much more than what you see.

As we learn to surrender our need to have answers for everything, may we find that by grace there is still room to go deep in the way that comes naturally to us. We may not know what lies ahead, but we know that we have spent time studying and preparing. And even though we can never fully prepare for life's unknown circumstances . . .

Yes, there is time for us to go on the back deck and breathe in the fresh morning air. There are books on the shelves to be read. There is space to be fully present with renewed energy in a living room filled with people we love, and there is also space for contemplation, rest, sleep.

We do not have to be everywhere doing everything at once, and, perhaps, deep within, we know this. When we start to learn that our ability to conceptualize and look at things objectively can actually be the way we begin to let go of things, we move from detachment to non-attachment. We move from staying away from others and keeping them at a distance to bringing what we learned at a distance into the present moment—with others, in community, in the world. We come down from the mountain of mind back down to earth and share what we have found.

1 Timothy 4:14 says, "Do not neglect your gift." Likewise, let us use our gift for good. Let us be the ones who remember that while this life here on earth is temporary, we have the daily opportunity to be present in every moment.

God,
In a world where it is far too easy to feel that I am
not equipped,
help me to remember the ways in which you have
gifted me.
Teach me to use my strengths in ways that allow me
to grow in love for you and others.
Amen.

LOVE OVER FEAR

PERHAPS THE BEST WAY to begin this forty-day journey is to take a loving look at one of the greatest traps in life: fear. The fear that we will not have the energy or capacity to be who we are supposed to be in the world unless we acquire more knowledge and understanding. The fear that we are not as equipped as others. The fear that if we really allow ourselves to feel the depth of our emotions, it will be too much.

Fives are typically drawn to particular interests, and we seek to be well-versed in the things we study. Our fear is being incompetent or incapable, and we try to work through those fears by retreating within, going inside our minds and lingering there for a while. In relationships we can seem secretive or guarded because we fear letting people in too much. Deep within, there's a question of, *What if I'm not enough? What if I don't have enough energy or resources to be who they need me to be?*

That's just the beginning of the list of ways fear can manifest itself in my life. However, this is also true: love is greater than fear. Love comes from God, and "there is no fear in love" (1 John 4:18).

As a Five, I tend to get stuck in my head. Because my head is the part of my body that is furthest from the ground, it can soar up in the clouds, floating in the theoretical. Love is what reminds me that below my endless thoughts, my heart still beats. The ground is still beneath my feet. I am free to be present amid all uncertainty.

Love reminds me that even when I think I am lacking, there is still room to be generous. Despite a tendency to withhold details about myself and the nuances of what I'm studying, I know it is enormously beneficial to be transparent and open.

The Enneagram is teaching me to be open. Open not only to deeper knowledge, but also open to love. And not the kind of love that is conditional and expects me to be someone I'm not, but the love of Christ, which is perfectly capable of leading me and filling my heart when I don't feel capable myself.

The beautiful thing about this kind of love is that I don't have to have words for it. In the moments when I feel loved or am able to show love to someone else, I don't have to know why. I don't have to tell myself it's because I prepared myself with the right amount of knowledge. I can trust that love is infinite. And within infinite love, there is room for me to grow in knowledge, and also to trust that there is life to be lived beyond my fears, right here, right now.

God,
For all of my fears,
even the ones I have yet to fully articulate or find the
*   words for,*
help me to remember that far below my thoughts,
my heart still beats,
the ground is still beneath my feet,
and within your Infinite Love,
despite what I lack
and don't understand,
I am where I need to be.
In your Infinite Love,
I am where I need to be.
Amen.

What does fear look like in your mind?

What does love look like in your life?

EMBRACING
UNCERTAINTY

AS A FIVE, I TEND TO focus on *why*. I want to know why things are the way they are. If I observe a problem, I start searching for possibilities as to why it might be a problem in the first place. I often see this as getting to the root. Going beyond the branches, the leaves, and the base of the tree in search of the thing that makes the problem itself make a little more sense. If I want to truly understand something, I want to go below the surface and find out what's really happening.

While this is an incredibly valuable skill in problem solving and troubleshooting, we Fives also need to be careful. We are in a healthier place when we realize that the roots we are digging up are lined with grace. It is okay to make connections and new discoveries, and it is also okay to say, "I don't know. . . . I don't have an answer for this."

It is okay to wonder why. It is also okay to fall in love with the act of digging and searching for answers. But may we do this while also trying to "love the questions themselves," as poet Rainer Maria Rilke says. May we realize that in grace, we are free to embrace uncertainty. We can fall in love with searching. Not just searching for answers, but searching for all the ways to fall in love with the mystery. To fall in love with learning whatever it is God wants us to learn. Even though the details have yet to be revealed to us, there is grace for us to be fully present with the questions.

Grace is an unmerited favor that gives us freedom to experience the peace of God even when we fall short of finding a solution. When we reach the inevitable edge of our knowledge and we've dug down to the deepest root we can reach, grace reminds us that it is okay if we do not feel we are good enough.

> But he said to me, "My grace is sufficient for you, for my power is made perfect in weakness." Therefore I will boast all the more gladly about my weaknesses, so that Christ's power may rest on me. (2 Corinthians 12:9)

On the other side of every question mark, may we continue to remember that grace will meet us there. Whether or not we find answers or get to the bottom of what we are searching for, we are not worth any less in the eyes of God. Our identity has not been lost. Amid all we do not know, this is still true: we are allowed to ask questions and we are still loved—even when we cannot find the answers.

God,
Oh, what a gift it is
to bask in your Presence,
a place where there is grace and wide open space
to ask questions my heart so desperately craves to
    know the answers to,
and all while I am searching, I get lost in you,
discovering that with or without the answers
    I feel like I need to have,
in the arms of your Love, I am free to
    experience peace
no matter the distance of my wonder, no matter the
    depths of my uncertainty.
In Christ, I am free to embrace the mystery of who
    you are
and all of the lessons and beautiful things you will
    continue to unfold before me.
Amen.

What question would you love to ask God today?

TURN AND FOLLOW THE SUN

IN ORDER TO GROW, THE SUNFLOWER knows it must turn its face to the sun. As Merrit Kennedy reported on NPR.org, the sunflower has an internal clock that helps it find daylight in the same way we humans naturally navigate our way through sleep-wake cycles. One of the fascinating things about the sunflower is that it learns to track the sun from east to west before it has fully bloomed, while it is still mostly green. Deep in the night it turns its face back east, where it gets ready to start the cycle again.

As a Five, I feel like I'm never quite ready. Even while writing this reflection I wonder if I have done my research properly or if I am qualified to share my thoughts. I often feel that in order to face the light of the day in a fully present way, I have to study and prepare a little more. I tell myself lies such as:

- "If I could understand the dynamics of my community a little bit more, maybe I would finally be able to relax and feel more present at social gatherings."

- "If I listen to this series of podcasts on families and parenting, then I will be equipped to be a better wife and mother."

- "If I spend the next few days withdrawn from social situations, then I'll have enough energy for the big event at the end of the week."

- "If I study the effects of this particular health challenge, then I'll finally be able to make sense of what I'm experiencing."

I forget that like the sunflower, I was meant to be awake and fully alive in broad daylight even before I'm ready. I forget that even though my mind tells me I need to withdraw and hang back until I feel a little more equipped, God has already equipped me with a body to follow the sun. I don't have to wait until I'm older and wiser. I don't have to wait until I have made my way through every book on my shelf. I don't have to familiarize myself with the social dynamics of a group before I can be present in that community and join in on the laughter. I am free to go out and be in the sun.  I am free to be a part of the lightheartedness and experience the presence of light-woven love, even if I don't understand it.

Light is sweet,
and it pleases the eyes to see the sun. (Ecclesiastes 11:7)

May we as Fives find pleasure in following the sun even before we feel ready. May those pockets of our mind that tell us we're not yet ready fail to keep us from being present to the grace that is sufficient for us.

Take heart; breathe deep. God has already readied your soul to turn to the sun. You are more prepared than you think.

God,
When I do not feel equipped,
lead my weary mind into remembering:
You have already given me what I need to be present
   to this life.
Teach me to follow the sun, from east to west, all
   throughout my days,
even when I do not feel I have what it takes.
In Christ, I will experience sufficient grace
to carry on faithfully toward whatever it is you have
   for me.
Even before I think I am ready.
Amen.

How can you turn and follow the sun today?

Who might you be able to talk to that you don't usually talk to?

Where might you go that you do not naturally feel compelled to go?

THE GIFT OF SOLITUDE

AS A FIVE, I FEEL THAT I am energized when I have time alone. One aspect of Jesus' life that has always resonated with me is the theme of solitude. Even before I discovered I was a Five, the thought of Jesus going off into a solitary place brought me a sense of peace. As a young one who grew up in a church culture where high-energy extroversion seemed to be the norm, I found myself cherishing Jesus' moments of solitude, which are woven throughout the Gospels. In times when I felt like I couldn't show up with a vibrant personality in the way some might expect, I clung to words like these:

> Very early in the morning, while it was still dark, Jesus got up, left the house and went off to a solitary place, where he prayed. (Mark 1:35)

While it is certainly true that Jesus spent adequate time with others, I love that this is also true: Jesus made room for solitude. Jesus made time to go away.

My prayer as a Five is that I can learn to retreat into solitude not out of fear of having inadequate inner resources but to simply spend time in the presence of God. To wake up in the early hours of the morning, open to what God longs to reveal to me on that day. Closing the door and going into a quiet place does not mean you are closed off from God's love.

This is something I long for every young Five to know. Young Fives often feel intruded upon by the outside world. In our childhood, we frequently felt overwhelmed and unsafe. We longed for private space, but it was hard to find. We craved solitude, but many interpreted this as being too closed off.

Even as we grow older, others may still interpret our behavior this way. But though we may be prone to withdraw from the world in a way that isn't healthy, let us continue to see God in the way Jesus did, to see solitude as a way of connecting to God.

Here's what's also true about solitude: we do not have to walk out of it with a new skill or something we've learned that we're ready to finally share with others. In the solitude, we are free to just be. When we come back into the world, we are still free to just be. Be present. Be a beacon of light. Be an example of love. Even if we don't know what to say or we can't figure out how we fit into a particular scenario, we can trust that God loves and guides us through our moments with others—and our moments alone.

God,
Thank you for giving me the gift of solitude.
Thank you for allowing me to have space to
contemplate and listen for your Voice.
I oftentimes feel overwhelmed by the world, and I
grateful that in Christ,
I am strengthened and I am renewed.
Thank you for the gift of community with others,
and also, communion with you, even in solitude.
Amen.

Where do you find solitude? Describe the place.

**What do you think eight-year-old you would think
about this space?**

REFILLING THE JAR

IF YOU OBSERVE WATER in a glass jar on a table, it is perfectly still and contained. Right there in the glass, the same liquid that forms the ocean is controlled and unmoved, sitting before you. Now imagine the jar gets tipped over. Suddenly the water goes from being controlled and contained to wild and free, ruining the book it's sitting next to and splattering all over the ground.

Like water in a glass jar, I am often more at ease when I feel a sense of control. The water outside the jar is wild and unpredictable, and it sends my heart racing as I try to clean it all up. As a Five, I find that this desire for control comes into play when I feel in need of safety and security. My mind is filled to the brim with ideas, my heart is liquid with emotions, but outside the jar of my home office or the confines of my journal, sharing this part of myself feels too dangerous and risky. I become overwhelmed by all the possible ways my thoughts might go spilling on to the floor.

The reason I feel this way is that Fives tend to have lower energy levels than other types. We need time to recharge before we rejoin others. However, it can be challenging for

Fives to figure out when they have been recharged enough. It can be difficult to find the courage to let the water spill out of private reserve into the flow of life. We fear that we won't be able to keep up with everyone else. We think that the longer we're outside the safety of our jars, the less energy we will have to sustain ourselves.

I have grown anxious many times thinking about the energy I'm not going to have left after taking a hike, going to an event, or making a presentation. However, time and again, I come back home and I recharge. Slowly but surely, water begins to fill that empty energy jar. And even when I am tempted to keep it to myself, I remember all the times God has shown me I am more capable of being out in the world than I think. Over and over, despite my fears of running out of energy and not having enough resources, I step out of my comfort zone and God surprises me. "My cup overflows" (Psalm 23:5).

I am reminded that all along, it was never up to me to try to manage and control everything. In God, I have what I need. And there, in God's divine presence, I become more than capable to show up in the way I am meant to.

God,
I praise you for filling my cup.
Thank you for reminding me over and over:
what you provide for me is more than enough.
Amen.

NEVER USELESS

I REMEMBER BEING IN my twenties, newly married, broke, and looking hopelessly at my résumé. In a few short years I had managed to work my way through a variety of jobs, drop out of grad school, and move to a new city with my husband where we didn't know anyone, bringing along a mountain of student loan debt.

All around me I was reminded of what I didn't know and what I wasn't capable of doing. I felt like I was unhirable, which led to a deeper feeling of uselessness. Even though I had spent years trying new things, building relationships, and growing in wisdom, it didn't seem like much when it was time to pay the bills.

One evening, all of the emotions that had been building up came flooding out from within and into the journal laid out before me. I lamented my fears and doubts in the form of a poem. I hadn't written poetry in years, but in that moment it felt like God was speaking through me as I wrote.

My poem was full of vulnerability and I was a little scared to show it to anyone, but somehow I ended up sharing it. It ended up becoming an example of grace in my life. It opened the door for me to share my story and help others dealing with similar feelings. I went from feeling completely unqualified and useless to feeling unqualified but aware that I was being used by God.

In Acts 18 we meet a woman named Priscilla. Born a Roman Jew, she became a Christian and began teaching about Jesus with her husband, Aquila. Culturally, there were many things Priscilla would not have been able to do in Rome, especially in a public role. However, as a follower of Christ, Priscilla was not useless. From hosting the apostle Paul in her home to training Apollo in the full teachings of Jesus, there was room for her: "[Apollo] began to speak boldly in the synagogue. When Priscilla and Aquila heard him, they invited him to their home and explained to him the way of God more adequately" (Acts 18:26).

I'm not sure what Priscilla's résumé looked like prior to assuming her role as a teacher of apostles, but I do know this: despite what her culture said she couldn't be, in Christ, she was so much more.

One of the basic fears of the Five is the fear of being useless. We fear that unless we are properly equipped in all the right ways, we won't be able to rise to the occasion. Priscilla is an example that no matter who sees us as less-than, we are not useless.

Our roles may change over the years, but we do not lose value when they do. In grace there is room for us to be honest about our fears while simultaneously being used by God in a meaningful way.

> *God,*
> *Today I come into your Presence*
> *with an open mind*
> *to how I might be used for good.*
> *I trust that far beyond what I know,*
> *or what I have believed about myself,*
> *I am not less than others.*
> *I am not useless.*
> *I am being equipped every day*
> *in Love,*
> *to do meaningful work, in grace.*
> *Amen.*

GUIDED: AN INVITATION

THINK ABOUT THE WAY your heart beats, and how it continues to beat even when you are tired. Even when you feel overwhelmed by the world around you, how beautiful it is that God has kept you alive, your heart expanding and contracting a hundred thousand times in one day alone. Reflect on this—even when you tread through uncertain waters.

Trust that even in these unknowns, you are being guided. You do not have to have all the answers. You do not need to have language for every feeling. You are free to just be in the presence, trusting that grace is more than enough.

When you pass through the waters,
    I will be with you;
and when you pass through the rivers,
    they will not sweep over you.
When you walk through the fire,
    you will not be burned;
    the flames will not set you ablaze. (Isaiah 43:2)

Though your heart may be tired and your spirit may be weak, you are free to keep going. Even though you pass through waters you do not know and even though there are far too many times when you feel like the ground might give out beneath you, God is with you. Your soul is protected.

When you don't feel like you are at your strongest and you can't figure out how to show up with the level of energy people seem to expect of you, hold on to truth: God is breathing life into your mind, body, and heart in every moment. Breathe deep and be present. Let this glorious presence do the rest.

There is no river you will cross and no fire you will walk through that will overtake you. Even there your soul will be steady. Even here, Christ-love will find you.

Trust. Believe. You are guided through these waters. May every heartbeat remind you of one more step you have taken on this grace-filled journey, even when you are tired.

> God,
> As I pass through the rivers,
> and walk through the fire,
> may I learn to trust in you.
> How marvelous it is to know
> I do not have to know how to travel through this
>   perfectly
> before I can lean into your perfect grace.
> Amen.

When you think about the way your heart beats, what words come to mind?

SUDDENLY, A LIGHT

A FEW YEARS AGO I had the opportunity to visit the Old City in Jerusalem. As I stood at the Damascus Gate, I was reminded of a verse that has always stood out to me. On his journey to Damascus, Paul—still Saul at the time—encountered Jesus in a life-altering way: "As he neared Damascus on his journey, suddenly a light from heaven flashed around him" (Acts 9:3).

Considering all that transpired in Paul's life after this event, this passage has long been a divine reminder to me of what is true in my own life: no matter what happens, it will be different when the light pours in. In reading this story of conversion, I have often imagined what it would be like to suddenly see the light of Jesus flash before your eyes. I have contemplated how equally beautiful and terrifying this moment must have been, like a lightning strike, leaving you with no choice but to slow down, grow silent, and listen, thus changing the course of your life.

However, on that hot, dry day in Jerusalem on a June afternoon, as I stood at the ancient gate, I realized there was something missing in this story of the Damascus journey I had been painting in my head. I had been on a tour of the Old City for several hours at this point, and I was starting to feel my energy levels dropping. As much as I was enjoying my time there, I had a strong desire to go back to the hotel, but the tour had a few more hours before it was time to head back. The liminal space was wearing on me, and now my mind was fixed on getting to sit down and rest, just to make it to a destination. It was in the moment that I began to reflect on how Paul, too, was just trying to get to his destination. He wasn't on an aimless journey searching for a divine revelation or a new direction in life. This encounter with light was an interruption, and it was also profoundly inconvenient. As I yawned and checked the time, I asked myself, *What if heaven flashed before me right now? Would I be ready? Or would I be too tired or overwhelmed by the interruption?*

I love a good journey where I am not in a hurry and free to travel at my own pace. However, as I stood there, ready to leave the Old City and recharge, I realized that it's often the unexpected parts of the journey where I encounter divine light. The moments in my life where I have been stopped in my tracks and forced to pay attention to what God was trying to show me have often been in liminal spaces where I'm just trying to get to my destination—a quiet place where I can recharge.

In Jerusalem, staring in the direction that leads to Damascus, I was reminded that the divine encounters I longed for in life might find me in the most inconvenient moments. The lessons I was meant to learn might not happen in the comfort of my reading chair, a cup of coffee, and a favorite book. Instead, I might just be called to grow in wisdom far out of my comfort zone—outdoors, far away from home, in a crowded, liminal space.

If I wanted to suddenly see a light in the way Paul did, I was going to have to bravely open my heart to learn what I was meant to learn even before I reached where I wanted to be. I was going to have to breathe deep and trust light will find me even before my energy is restored. And this is how I will truly begin to grow in wisdom. This is where I will experience transformation.

> Think of a place you have traveled that you will always remember. Perhaps it strikes you for its historical relevance, its beauty, or the peace you found there. This place can be many miles away or a few streets away from you. Using all of your available senses, reflect on the things you remember about this place. Write down what you think God may have been teaching you there.

FROM CONCEPT
TO ACTION

ON OUR SPIRITUAL JOURNEY as Fives, we may crave contemplative moments that allow us to retreat into our minds and reflect on the stories and ideas that help us understand the path we're on. We may look to ancient wisdom to better equip ourselves with knowledge in hopes to understand and feel a sense of safety. For me, this often means imagining how someday I will finally travel to places where I will find a sense of peace. It all started with the maps folded up in the glove compartment of my parent's old Volvo. I used to unfold them and trace my finger over the nearest river and wonder what it would take to get there. I would follow the course of the interstate we traveled every day and look for the creeks and footpaths on the other side of the Georgia pine trees that lined the road. As I've gotten older and technologically has improved, I've been able to expand beyond the local maps, scrolling my way over the rock formations of Meteora, Greece, where monasteries are carved all the way into the rocks' edges. These days, I'm tracing my mouse over the coastlines of Madagascar, imagining what it might be like to rest by those shores.

Imagination is a powerful force, and sometimes the sheer thought of traveling to a place brings me a sense of peace. However, like I soon discovered with the maps in the Volvo, maps only take me so far. Eventually, they must go back into the glove department and it's time to get on the road. That's when I'll discover that the journey is lined with spaces for quiet moments away from it all, if I allow myself to look for them. All along the path, there are rest stops, book shops, and benches in the park. I may not always be able to travel the unbridled path to the deep river in the woods, or hop on a plane to visit a monastery peering over the city, but I can look for the gold in the present moment. I can still put the map aside for a while and dare to exist in spaces where I feel welcomed and free.

As Fives, it can be challenging to turn our thoughts into action even when it comes to things we *want* to do. As Don Riso and Russ Hudson write in *Wisdom of the Enneagram,* we "are most effective when [we] stop refining concepts and actually get into action." Fives tend to "collapse into preparation mode" and I believe we can get stuck in this mode even when it comes to things we actually want to do, such as traveling to a far-off, peaceful destination. Thinking it through comes naturally to us. For us, the journey doesn't begin when the map goes back into the glove department, but long before . . . taking as much time as we need to trace our fingers over the map.

As we seek to explore from a distance, may we always remember that the map is a symbol depiction of a place and not the place itself. We can learn a lot from observing this complex network of roads and rivers and mountain scapes, and at the same time, these places exist off the paper. Every day, we have the opportunity to turn the keys in the ignition and go exploring, with or without the map. We are allowed to be curious in public. We are free to be observers out in the open.

We are free to go beyond the boundaries of what you know. The journey is calling.

> *God,*
> *Teach me to be present to endless ways that Jesus might show up in my life today.*
> *Fill my heart with courage and awareness of you so that I may not be afraid.*
> *When I reach that place in my mind, searching for comfort in what I know,*
> *desperately trying to prepare for whatever is to come,*
> *may your abundant grace remind me to open my heart to the possibility of how I might be surprised and shaped by you.*
> *Amen.*

PLAYING THE PART

I HAVE RUN INTO SITUATIONS where people who are familiar with the Enneagram are surprised to learn that I am a Five. Based on stereotypes, some assume Fives don't have feelings or know how to engage with the world. Even though I am introverted, I have learned the ropes of presenting as an extrovert.

Ever since I was a kid, I have found myself in a lot of high-energy communities where if I planned on keeping up, especially socially, I had to be vocal and outspoken. I learned to study the social cues of my peers and even mimic mannerisms and facial expressions. I would listen to whatever music was trending with that group so I could blend in. I even taught myself to play guitar so I could be useful when hanging out.

I learned how to play the part. I learned that if I wanted to be heard or seen, I had to show up like everyone else. I was rarely anxious about this when I was in the moment, and I would methodically work my way through. But when I got home, I was exhausted. It would take me a day or two to fully recover the energy I had exerted trying to keep up with everyone else.

As with all types, we Fives have our limitations, and these are often centered around the amount of energy we have to give. However, having limitations does not mean we are incapable. When we become aware of our limits, we find freedom. Finally, we can breathe deep and say, "This is what I have to give today." And that's okay.

If I could tell my college-age self anything, it would be the words above. I would tell her there is nothing wrong with stepping out of your comfort zone to cultivate connection, but if you're not always up to it, that's okay. If you need some alone time instead of going out with the group, take that time and don't worry about it.

Whether you consider yourself to be a more social Five or not, may you always remember to take care of yourself by making room to breathe. If there's only so much gas in the tank today, accept it. You do not have to exhaust yourself trying to keep up with everyone else. You do not have to play the part because it feels like it's what you *should* do. Even in public settings, you are allowed to be quiet. You don't have to put on a show.

Blessed are the meek,
    for they will inherit the earth. (Matthew 5:5)

> **When have you had to "play the part" recently? Who can you share this experience with?**

OPEN SPACE

IF YOU HAVE EVER TRAVELED a long distance on a highway, at some point you have likely found spaces where the land opened up into a large area that seemed to stretch for miles and miles. Free of forests and cities, the land at first glance didn't seem to offer much to see.

However, in spaces like these, the longer you look, the more you find. The landscape is filled with diverse textures, colors, and life forms. It is alive. Even beneath the ground, the soil carries a rich history all its own. Though it at first seems boring or uninteresting, you realize this land is creating an unforgettable spaciousness that affects you, even when you look from a distance.

Fives have the gift of detachment. This does not mean we stand at a distance, aloof. Instead it means we have a way of looking at the whole landscape without becoming attached to one particular blade of grass, or string of clouds, or point of view. We take into consideration what the field looks like from every angle. From above, below, east to west. We take it all in.

Psalm 18:36 reads, "You provide a broad path for my feet, so that my ankles do not give way." What a glorious thought to think of God opening up the space beneath our feet, creating a wide distance from side to side, far beyond what even a trained eye can see. This path leads us to grow not only in knowledge but also in the love of God.

As we Fives travel down the highways of unknowns in life, may we remember that we have the ability to look back at the whole landscape in a thoughtful way. And on that broad path, God meets us. When we reach the end of what we know, God does not abandon us.

> *God,*
> *In wide open spaces,*
> *may I remember that you are close.*
> *In an unbroken expanse*
> *of known or unknown lands,*
> *with every pace I can trust:*
> *I am guided. I am seen.*
> *You will reveal to me what is meant to be revealed*
>   *to me.*
> *Amen.*

What does an open field tell you about your view of the world and also your faith?

SUBMERGED SUNRISE
OF WONDER

AS FIVES, WE LIKE TO BE PREPARED. In fact, we often feel like we are never finished preparing. There's always another layer to dig down into. There's always another question that opens up a hundred more. But the truth is, we can prepare only so much—and then there is a point when we look to the horizon in all of its beauty and accept that we do not know what lies beyond it.

We learn to trust that even when we do not feel prepared, we are often more prepared than we realize. Our lives are filled with experiences that have led to this one. We may not be able to consciously recall every single thing we have learned and lived through, but we trust that the knowledge is there. We have the strength and wisdom to carry on, even if we do not know what waits on the other side.

G. K. Chesterton writes in his autobiography, "At the back of our brains, so to speak, there [is] a forgotten blaze or burst of astonishment at our own existence. The object of the artistic and spiritual life [is] to dig for this submerged sunrise of wonder."

May we never forget what rests beneath the layers, under the water. Even when we have to walk up to the platform and speak before we've done enough research. Even when we enter a new relationship and there is still so much to learn about this person. Even when we acknowledge the stirring within our hearts to take the leap, and yet we are afraid of jumping too soon. These fears are real, but so is grace.

Grace reminds us that far beyond our memory, we are stronger than we think. We are more equipped to travel

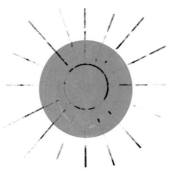

toward the horizon than we can articulate. Perhaps our souls know more than our minds do. Perhaps the "forgotten blaze" is still burning, even when we are helplessly trying to acquire new knowledge to start a new fire. Maybe the horizon we are looking at is an invitation to remember that though we travel new unknowns, God is with us.

Our anxieties about the unknowns in our lives may seem ever-present, but I hope you know that peace is ever present too. So take heart. Breathe in. And let that breath go. Let go of your expectations of how you think the future should be. Let this be a season of surrendering, trusting, and believing that no matter what tomorrow looks like, no matter what does or does not go according to plan, you are still on the journey. You are looking toward the horizon, finding that on the other side of it, life is still meaningful and filled with wonder.

> He marks out the horizon on the face of the waters
> for a boundary between light and darkness.
>> (Job 26:10)

God,
Thank you for giving me a mind that is free to imagine.
May I use my imagination to visualize not just
scenarios and concepts,
but also how Divine Love may show up in my
life today.
Guide me in remembering I am more than my mind.
Even when I can't figure things out, I am still on
a journey,
and I am free to lean in toward the horizon, with
hope for what is to come,
without fear and worry that I am enough.
In Love, I am enough.
Amen.

NEVER SEPARATED

FIVES GROW WHEN WE soften into trusting that our ability to look at things from a distance does not mean we are separate from the world, other people, or the love of God. Our ability to theorize and look at things from an objective point of view does not mean we do not get to show up as our unique selves with others and also before God.

There have been many moments in my life when I have been the wallflower. Friends and well-meaning strangers alike have walked up to me at social gatherings and asked, "Are you okay?" They ask because I'm not out on the dance floor "joining in on the fun" or participating in the activities. In those situations, it is difficult and sometimes even impossible to explain that I am actually enjoying myself. I enjoy watching from the small distance where I am standing. Even then, I am still in the room. I am present.

As Fives, we do not have to stay away, cut off from everyone else just because we relate to the world in a different way. We are free to be present and experience connection and community and fully engage in whatever lessons God has for us in that moment. We can still make an effort to go out and let others in without thinking we need to change our personality. We are free to live this life up close, just like everyone else.

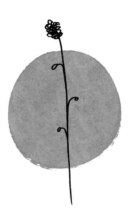

Detachment does not mean distance. Cerebral does not mean separate. We are still connected. We are still a part of the bigger picture. The greater story is this: "Neither height nor depth, nor anything else in all creation, will be able to separate us from the love of God that is in Christ Jesus our Lord" (Romans 8:39).

> *God,*
> *Reveal to me the ways*
> *I can be perceptive while not neglecting*
> *   participation,*
> *detached but not distant.*
> *I am fearfully and wonderfully made by you.*
> *For all I know and yearn to know,*
> *your Divine awareness of me*
> *goes beyond what I can see,*
> *so I trust you.*
> *I trust you to lead me into a daily surrender*
> *where I let go of my inclination to separate and stay*
> *   at a distance.*

I praise you for all you are,
and all you are to me,
including the Strong One,
who strengthens me to join in whatever you want
    me to join,
in the way you have uniquely equipped me to do so
in Christ.
Amen.

Journal about a moment when you managed to make it through a social gathering or event that you thought would overwhelm you. How did God meet you that day?

FAITH TO LET GO

OVER AND OVER, I AM LEARNING to let go. I am learning to loosen my grip and trust in the midst of the unknown, entirely unaware of what God will do.

Jochebed, mother of Moses, is an example of someone who literally had to let go in pursuit of the unknown. She had no idea what future awaited her young son when she placed him in a papyrus basket and sent him down the Nile river. All she knew was that the Egyptians were killing the male sons of Hebrew slaves, and her son's only chance at survival was for him to be away from her. The Scripture text reads, "But when she could hide him no longer, she got a papyrus basket for him and coated it with tar and pitch. Then she placed the child in it and put it among the reeds along the bank of the Nile" (Exodus 2:3).

We do not know what Jochebed felt that day as she sent her young baby down the river, but we do know that she was a woman of strong faith. It takes faith to let go and trust that God will make something of the unknowns.

As Fives, we encounter times when the unknown calls our names. We feel compelled to go deeper and further into knowledge and understanding. But there are also times when in order to embrace the unknown, we have to let go. We have to surrender the way we thought things would be in exchange for uncertainty.

Even if God does something miraculous with the unknown, as he did in the life of Jochebed's son Moses, that doesn't mean we will get to see how it all plays out. There are many mysteries in this life that we might not live to see solved. But God is still working. The river is still flowing. We learn to make the hard decision of loosening our grip and we trust that God will do something far beyond what we can see.

Where can you practice letting go today? Who can you share this part of your journey with?

ETERNAL FLAME

ABOUT FORTY MILES SOUTH of Niagara Falls on the US side, tucked away in the Shale Creek Preserve, there's a much smaller waterfall called Eternal Flame Falls. It gets its name from a rare natural occurrence at the falls' base, where a small flame burns just behind the curtain of falling water. Geologists have been studying the emission of natural gas at the base of this waterfall for years. It is a beautiful phenomenon (and definitely worth a quick internet search to see for yourself!).

When I stumbled on an article about this natural mystery, I couldn't believe I knew nothing about it when I visited Niagara Falls a few years ago. Anytime I visit a new place, I always look at a map of the surrounding area, especially nearby parks and reserves. While I cherish my experience at Niagara, I was disappointed to learn that I could have easily gone just a little farther south to see the Eternal Flame. However, like many other tourists, I was caught up in the shine of the main attraction. I was completely unaware of the smaller yet more rare falls down the road.

This caused me to think of all of the other moments in my life when my attention was captivated by the main attraction, yet somewhere down the road there may have been something more rare that I missed.

Perhaps I am drawn to this thought because I often feel a bit like the rare waterfall, a little farther south down the less traveled path. Burning with creativity and connection, fascinated by the infinite, I create rhythms of going deeper and deeper into knowledge every day. I flicker and I flicker.

Unlike Niagara, there's no LED light show every night. No fireworks or boat tours. Buried in the forest, my energy is quieter, reserved.

And that's okay. I am free to flicker on anyway. Niagara Falls is a beautiful, natural wonder, and I am divinely created all the same.

As Fives, we have a natural curiosity that sends us down narrow paths of very specific and rare interests. While this journey brings us enjoyment, it can also at times make us feel a little lonely, left wondering, *Is there a place in the world for me?* We end up missing flickers of connection in the same way we feel like people have failed to notice us.

We may not naturally attract everyone's attention like the more noticeable falls up the road, but we are certainly not alone in this world. The psalmist writes, "My frame [is] not hidden from you" (Psalm 139:15).

The flame still burns from within. Tucked in the forest of our mind, the light is still radiant. We have the flickering rhythm of something beautiful and never forgotten by God, even down the less traveled paths.

> *God,*
> *I am so grateful that my frame is not hidden*
>   *from you.*
> *I am so grateful that even in my quiet place,*
> *tucked away from the busyness and rush of life,*
> *off the beaten path,*
> *in a place where everyone doesn't see,*
> *you have set a fire within me.*
> *Thank you for being present*
> *down the narrows where my mind leads me.*
> *Thank you for revealing that even in that place,*
> *I am whole.*
> *I am filled with Life.*
> *Amen.*

What lesser-known natural wonder has caught your attention? What do you love about it? What could it teach you about yourself?

TRUST YOUR BODY

WITHIN THE NINE TYPES of the Enneagram, there are three lenses through which we tend to perceive the world: head, heart, and body. These are called the triads. As Ian Morgan Cron and Suzanne Stabile write in *The Road Back to You,* the triads represent how we "habitually take in, process, and respond to life."

Fives lead with thought, perceiving the world most dominantly through our heads. While this is a strength, it also presents a challenge—we can find it difficult to be present in our bodies. At times we are more prone to study the ground beneath our feet than to take our shoes off to see how it feels. Our knowledge of the ocean tends to come more from observation than diving in.

This is not at all to say the Five never acts. I personally love playing instruments and hiking through canyons, both of which are very bodily experiences. However, more often than not, I find it easier to get into my head than my body.

As I have become more aware of these tendencies, I have slowly but surely begun to realize that my inner work as a

Five is going to take some outer work as well. If I want to grow, I am going to grow from the ground up.

When I feel lost in the wilderness of my thoughts, I can study the map for only so long before it's time to take the actual steps to get home. I can study the flowers and reach down to smell them too. I can find peace in reflecting on the openness of the sky and also go open the nearest window and feel the wind on my skin. I can think about how I'd like to make deeper connections with friends and I can also bravely choose to pick up the phone when it rings.

Fives often feel pressure to be more active. While challenging yourself in this area can be an incredibly helpful practice, it is also true that there are infinite ways to be active. You can take the camping trip and also bring a book or two. You can go to the social gathering and also record your thoughts in your journal when you get home. You can open up to people who are close to you and share your interests with them, even if you feel like they won't get it or understand it. You can thank God for your body and also for your mind. In grace, there is room for who you naturally are and also who you can grow to be.

Getting into our bodies does not mean we have to neglect how we have been uniquely wired. What matters is that we remember there is always room for growth.

God,
Sometimes I feel lost because I am not sure how to
get into action.

*I struggle to connect with my body, and I feel
    incapable compared to others.*

*These struggles often send me inward and they keep
    me from connecting with others.*

They keep from connecting with you.

Amid all the pressure I feel to be active,

*may I remember that with every step I take, even the
    small ones,*

there is grace.

*I do not have to try to be active the way everyone
    else is all in one day.*

*There is a place for me in the world as I have
    been created.*

*I do not have to change my personality to find my
    way home to you.*

*I only need to stay the course with a heart
    wide open,*

*trusting that what it is meant to be revealed will be
    revealed to me in time.*

I will grow, out here, on the road, in Love, with you.

Amen.

INFINITE: AN INVITATION

PRAY AN OPEN PRAYER. Pray a prayer that stretches over the horizon into the furthest fields and deepest voids of your mind.

You have long been in love with the concept of infinity. You long for infinite wisdom. So open your mind before God. Open it with full-color curiosity. Pray prayers with big questions. Pray the prayers you are not even sure how to say out loud.

God can hold them. God is infinite.

Say to God that you are willing to go into the depths. As sure as your late-night dreams take you to endless galaxies and over boundless seas, God's love is even more boundless. So ask the questions you can't ask anyone else. Even if you can't possibly imagine what the answers might be. Feel the beat of your heart as the words leave your lips.

God can hold them. God is infinite.

You have grown so weary of the ordinary. You have learned to hold what is good and beautiful here, but even the good things seem to have their own limitations. You feel the ground beneath your feet and it is real, but so is the sky above you. The mountains beyond you. And watching how their bases roll out across the landscape reminds you of eternity.

Why can't you just travel onward and onward toward eternity? You are grateful, but you want more. You want to wander into the open fields. You long to go deeper than ever before. But you feel stuck. And you struggle, wondering if you're enough. Perhaps what it matters is that you first decide you are going to take the risk. Ask God the big questions.

God can hold them. God is infinite.

You have traveled the full range of what you're capable of, and you have started to realize that in order to grow, you need something greater than you. You are grateful for all you have learned here, but you are learning to see that this isn't all there is. Let yourself see this as a chance to be free. A chance to surrender the endless uncertainty for endless peace. Lay your questions down. Loosen your shoulders. You have carried so, so much. And now . . .

God will hold them. God is infinite and you are infinitely loved.

Call to me and I will answer you and tell you great and unsearchable things you do not know. (Jeremiah 33:3)

When you hear, "You are infinitely loved," what comes to mind? A galaxy? An ocean? A special moment in your life? How do you feel in your body when you hear these words?

EMBRACING
THE SILENCE

AS FIVES, WE ARE NATURALLY PRONE to want to figure things out. We are driven to understand and we will search long and hard for answers. When it comes to the big unknowns in our lives, may we continue to assume a posture of surrender. May we choose to identify where and how to let go.

Perhaps we can give up the internet search engine for a day. Maybe we can choose music over a podcast to help calm our mind. And from there, perhaps, we can have an encounter with silence, knowing that God meets us even where there are no words. In *Listening for God*, Renita J. Weems writes, "What if God's silence was not a ruse? What if God's silence is precisely the way God speaks?"

Sometimes I look for God in the same way I look for answers. I try to connect the dots and draw lines between concepts. But over and over again, I am reminded that God is not restricted to words on a page or the connections I can make. I am reminded how God left me speechless at the

Grand Canyon. I am reminded how I felt close to him during the hailstorm when I was jobless and in a quarter-life crisis.

God has shown me again and again that silence keeps me open. Silence keeps me listening. If all I ever hear is noise, and if every single moment I must have a book open or a philosophy to fall back on, then I won't be able to trust. And if I can't trust, I can't let go. And if I can't let go, I won't grow.

> *God,*
> *And, oh, how beautifully you allow room for plants*
>   *to grow*
> *by the window*
> *even in the waiting seasons.*
> *The sun finds its way in*
> *and I remember*
> *to water them,*
> *and somehow,*
> *this is more than enough.*
> *Amen.*

OVERWHELMED BY EVERYTHING

WHEN I WAS TWO YEARS OLD, my mother asked me what I wanted for Christmas. As the story goes, I took a deep breath, dramatically tossed my hands into the air and, with a mixture of excitement and overwhelm, exclaimed, "Everything!"

For many years I was perplexed by this story. I don't recall wanting very much during my childhood—especially not "everything." And as I discovered the Enneagram in my twenties, the story confused me even more. What did it say about me, a woman who prides herself on not wanting or needing very much?

I thought of my younger self, overwhelmed by the options presented to me. I imagine flipping through one of those old JCPenney catalogs and looking at the photographs, unable to decide. What was my little heart saying when she exhaled, "Everything"?

Ecclesiastes 3:1 says, "There is a time for everything, and a season for every activity under the heavens." This popular verse has been quoted and shared for just about—

well, everything. After hearing it many times, I read through the entire chapter of Ecclesiastes 3, and as I read I was reminded of all the things human beings must hold during our time under the heavens: planting and uprooting, searching and giving up, mourning and dancing, weeping and laughing, embracing and refraining, giving birth and dying—everything. I struggle to make sense of it all. I struggle to feel that I am competent or equipped to hold all the tragedies and gifts of the world in my mind.

But the beautiful thing is, I am slowly learning I don't have to. I am starting to see that I don't have to hold everything at once; I don't have to try to make sense of every single gift to be present to what I am meant to learn in this life. I am learning, in the words of Teresa of Ávila, "to have courage for whatever comes in life—everything lies in that."

To try to hold and make sense of everything at once is an impossible feat, but when I realize there is a time for everything, that all things eventually pass, I find rest. Even when I reach my limits, my heart still bends toward eternity. I am free to breathe deep and find infinite peace for everything.

> *God,*
> *When my mind is overwhelmed by everything,*
> *help me to come back down from the high hills of*
>   *my endless thoughts*
> *and into this present moment,*
> *so that I may be present, at home with you.*
> *Amen.*

Read Ecclesiastes 3:1-8 out loud to yourself. How do you feel in your body when reading these words? Does anything come up in your heart? Journal your thoughts.

FOR SUCH A TIME AS THIS: AN INVITATION

NO MATTER WHO YOU HAVE looked at and deemed more worthy or more important than you, trust this: you are worth no less. God has given you a voice even if your words come out differently. You may feel the length of the distance between yourself and others, but you are still connected. You are not cut off even when you struggle to keep up with the pace and demands of others.

I know it can feel like you are halfway through running a race and you feel your legs weakening, the heat of the concrete rising up below your feet—but even then, your heart still beats. Even then, there is room and air to breathe. There is room for you to bravely choose to continue on, even if you are moving at a pace that is slower or more careful than that of those around you.

Now is the time to live with wholehearted courage. Allow yourself to hold in your hands the reality of what is. But at the same time, ask the question, *God, what more do you have for me?* Let this question open up places in your heart that may have been closed off because intimacy and connection have been overwhelming to you. Let this prayer be a courageous act of trusting that God has more for you.

When King Xerxes came to power, he chose Esther, an Israelite, to be his wife. When a high-ranking political advisor sought to have the Israelites killed, Esther's cousin Mordecai spoke these words to her: "If you remain silent at this time, relief and deliverance for the Jews will arise from another place, but you and your father's family will perish. And who knows but that you have come to your royal position for such a time as this?" (Esther 4:14).

What position do you hold in your environment? Because of that position, who might you be able to speak to? Perhaps you have a gift of teaching. You may have observed that your teaching style is different from others', but your approach may just be what one student needs, even in a nonacademic setting. Who knows—maybe there's a little Five in the crowd who has been waiting to hear from someone like you.

Perhaps in your family or circle of friends you are known for having a very specific set of knowledge. This may cause you to feel isolated at times. But how can your knowledge serve others? How can your strengths in researching help someone you love find the resources they need?

It will take courage to show up in the lives of others in this way, but it's worth it. All along, you have been called to more. All along, this life has been about surrendering how we think we should be in the world in exchange for openness and willingness to grow.

Show up with courage today. Not with cleverness or perfection, and maybe not even with advice. Show up to listen. Show up to reflect those who do not see themselves reflected. Be present to those who are different from you and also to those who are like you. Perhaps you were made for such a time as this.

What part of Esther's story do you connect with the most? What internal challenges do you think she faced that you may have faced in your life as a Five?

THROUGH WALLS
OF WATER

AS A FIVE, I CAN FIND it difficult to articulate my emotions. However, that does not mean I do not have emotions. It often takes me much longer than others to process how I feel about something, but those feelings are still real.

I often feel the aliveness of my emotions all the more when I am in solitude. While I am listening to music or reading a book, something as simple as musical notes arranged in a particular way or a words put together in a certain phrase can make me feel delighted or amused, or even afraid and unsettled. The wide range of emotions I feel can catch me by surprise, and at times I find myself wanting to avoid them. I struggle to walk through them for fear they may consume me.

I often wonder what crossed the minds of the Israelites as they walked through the parted Red Sea, escaping Egypt: "[They] went through the sea on dry ground, with a wall of water on their right and on their left" (Exodus 14:29). I wonder who might have stopped to look up at the walls of water and if they feared the flood of water consuming them. How on earth did they process what was happening in that moment?

I view my emotions this way. Intellectually, I know the emotions will pass and I will make it to the other side of them. But I can't help but wonder, *What if I don't make it in time? What if they consume me? What if all my emotions come crashing down before I reach the other side?*

In those moments I am overwhelmed by the possibility of getting lost. I fear I will lack the know-how to make it out of troubled waters. However, perhaps like the Israelites walking through the walls of the Red Sea, I will find that somehow I have made it to the other side of the emotion. Even with my feelings stacked high around me, threatening to crash down at any second, I still made it through.

When anguish and grief climb high around me, I am free to trust that there is a path toward exodus beneath my feet. I will face the unknowns of my emotions again and again, but I am free to trust that I am equipped for those moments. Despite walls of water on either side, I will make it through with God.

God,
There are times when my emotions feel like too much.
Like walls of water climbing high around me,
they may come crashing down and I will drown.
Help me to remember the path beneath my feet.
Help me to remember that I am not as lost as I
    thought I was.
The more I trust and the more I choose to stay
    present to this very moment,
The more I will be reminded that I am still on the path.
The emotions I feel will not last forever.
Thank you for grace that reminds me it is okay to feel.
Thank you for your constant reminders through
    the day
that I am so much more capable than I think.
Amen.

I'LL ASK GOD LATER

"HOW DO YOU KNOW GOD SPEAKS TO YOU?" my father asked me.

"When my brain says something so smart that I know I couldn't have thought of it myself."

This was how my six-year-old-preacher's-daughter self understood the voice of God. And to be honest, I still like to think that the brand new ideas that pop into my brain might just be God's way of speaking to me.

My father would often ask me curious questions like this, and I never hesitated to answer with assurance. Even when it came to more complex theological questions that usually began with, "Why does God . . . ," I casually shrugged it off, saying things like, "I don't know; I'll just ask God when I get to heaven. I'll ask him later." I had assurance. Even when it came to topics of great mystery, I somehow found it in me to be okay with the parts I didn't know.

While I have continued to think about God appearing to me in my thoughts, as I have gotten older, it has become harder to be okay with "asking God later." I developed the practice of working my way through long rows of book-shelves in my father's office and my own college library, but I still have had to accept that for some things, there are no easy answers.

Somehow, "asking God later" was replaced with flipping through pages, drawing connections, and trying to make sense of life's moments that you leave you wondering, *God, why did you let this happen?* No longer content with waiting, I resolved to try to figure it out. I would ask and I would ask, and eventually God would answer, right?

I hope that as I grow older (and hopefully wiser), my heart can continue to be open to what God will show me in the years to come. I hope that even though my mind wants the answers now, the patiently curious child within me can surrender and wait till later. The writer of Hebrews puts it this way: "Now faith is confidence in what we hope for and assurance about what we do not see" (Hebrews 11:1).

As the years go on, our questions lead us down the aisles of libraries, along the hallways of museums, and through endless digitally rendered encyclopedia pages. One curiosity quickly unfolds into a dozen others. We struggle to stay on top of things because we feel a gravitational force calling us to get to the bottom of things instead. We lose track of time and, inevitably, we reach our limits. In grace, we sink down into the reality that it's okay. It's okay to have questions. Some answers come only with time. As Zora

Neale Hurston writes, "There are years that ask questions and years that answer."

May we always remember to have faith beyond what we see, confident that high over our worries, in grace, we are free to slow down, breathe deep, and rest our heavy minds, for what is meant to be revealed to us will be revealed to us in time.

God,
Thank you for giving me this mind.
Thank you for the gift of wisdom.
Teach me today to lean into your All-Knowingness
more than I lean into my own understanding.
Give me strength to live with questions so that I
may trust that in the space between what I have
asked and your answer, there is abundant room
to grow in faith.
Amen.

What question are you asking God right now? Before writing it down or researching it, engage in a conversation with someone you can share this question with.

LOVE IS

HERE'S THE LIBERATING THING about love: within it, there is room for you to be who you are, and there is also room for growth. There is room to listen, observe, and learn from others and share your wisdom too. In short, in love, by grace, there is room.

As a Five, I have found the word *love* to be intimidating at times. Intellectually I understand it, but sometimes *love* feels like a warm, fuzzy feeling that I can't quite generate at the same speed as others. Knowing I need love, I begin to realize there is room to expand my definition. In studying the origin of the word *love* and what it looks like in other languages, I found myself on a rabbit trail that brought me back home to seeing that love is more than a feeling; love is a way of being. I can show love and be an example of love even when I don't feel equipped.

Parker Palmer writes, "The highest form of love is the love that allows for intimacy without the annihilation of difference."

Love is being present with one another.

Love is allowing room for difference.

Love is listening.

Love is serving.

Love is being the friend who helps solve the problem.

Life is being the friend who can't solve the problem but chooses to be present anyway.

Love is many things.

Love is harmony.

Live in harmony with one another. Do not be proud, but be willing to associate with people of low position. Do not be conceited. (Romans 12:16)

As a Five, I have at times fallen into the trap of thinking I understand what people are going to need from me. I end up exhausting the very energy I was trying to protect by overthinking all the questions someone might ask so I'll open up more. However, the passage from Romans reminds me that staying only in my head makes it harder for me to be in the room. I may be able to intellectually let myself float to the ceiling and just observe, but the ground is still beneath my feet. I still need to breathe. I still must be present to who is in front of me, whether in larger social settings or smaller, intimate settings.

Harmony is the act of bringing notes together. The notes can be different, but when played at the same time, they fill the room beautifully. The same is true when we are present, in the room, in love.

Complete the sentence, "Love is . . . "

What does love look like to you today?

WITH WINDOWS OPEN

AS FIVES, WE TEND TO PUT UP boundaries to create safe spaces for ourselves. This is especially true when we sense that something is about to go wrong. However, when we are overwhelmed, those boundaries can become stone walls that are hard to remove. In an unhealthy state, we can become closed off from the world, losing sight of the greater picture.

When Daniel, an advisor to King Darius in ancient Babylon, discovered that he would be thrown into the lions' den for worshiping God, "he went home to his upstairs room where the windows opened toward Jerusalem. Three times a day he got down on his knees and prayed, giving thanks to his God, just as he had done before" (Daniel 6:10).

Daniel was a wise man who was known for his intelligence; he even aided the king in interpreting dreams. However, even in his high position—he had risen from captive prisoner to leader next to the king—he continued to seek God above all, no matter what it cost.

In the comfort of his own home, he went upstairs where the windows were open. He stayed in rhythms of prayer and devotion to God, even when he knew the trouble that awaited him.

As Fives, may we remember to go where the window is open. May we remember that even when we face serious trouble, there is still room in that very moment to keep our hearts open to the fullness of who God is.

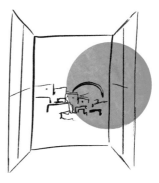

When Daniel looked out his window toward Jerusalem, he saw a place that was once home to his people only to be completely overthrown. He saw this as he was getting ready to face even more captivity. And yet still he found himself on his knees, in prayer, in total surrender.

What windows do you need to open emotionally? What windows can you open in the spaces you'll travel through today?

HUMILITY

WHEN I WAS YOUNGER, I went on a class trip to a nearby forest where we were to participate in team-building exercises before the semester officially began. The first exercise involved standing on a log and figuring out how to get everyone from one end of the log to the other. According to the rules, we couldn't simply walk off in a single-file line. Everyone had to cross paths with someone else on the log in some way before reaching the other side.

I stood on the log among six other students who quickly began trying to figure it out, many of them talking over one another, energetically trying to solve the problem. As the chatter grew louder, I remembered that years before, at another camp, I had done this exercise before, and I remembered the solution. I tried to get the attention of my classmates several times, but no matter how much I tried to speak up, no one heard me.

We literally just met, and here I am, already turning into the invisible one, I thought to myself.

Just as I had given up, the camp counselor cupped his hands and called out to all of us, "Hey! Everyone! One of your team members has been trying to get your attention for ten minutes—she's already done this exercise before and has insight, but no one is listening!"

Everyone grew quiet and listened to my instructions. In less than a minute, everyone was off the log, having crossed paths by crouching down and hopping over instead of trying to cross side by side.

For my awkward, introverted teenage self, this moment was like a dream. I had never experienced any other moment in life when I was not only heard, but also everyone followed my instructions and succeeded. My time had been well invested and I felt respected. I walked away from that experience thinking about how nice it would be to have a camp counselor follow me around and shout, "Hey! Pay attention to Morgan! She's got the answers! She knows how this works!"

However, as special as that moment was, it was rare. As it turns out, if I want to be heard, I have to speak up. Or I have to humbly let go of my desire to be the one who offers the solution. Even when I try to let go, though, I still struggle, wondering if I've wasted my time trying to help. I have to try not to let resentment grow within because of those who didn't listen.

In a perfect world, I would always have confidence that my time has not been wasted. I would spend all those hours researching or trying to help someone solve a problem and then watch it all come together seamlessly. But in this perfect world there would be no room to trust. There would be no room to go beyond my ego and pay attention to how God wants me to surrender.

The time I invest in others cannot be measured. The time I spend offering advice or helping others research must come from a place of wanting to act on love, not feeding my ego.

As Fives, we value time. But may we never view time invested as the way to measure worthiness or meaning in life. When we help others investigate an issue or give advice based on what we've studied, may we do so from a place of love and humility. May we practice surrender by letting go of the need to see how it all plays out. Let us remember how patient God is with us in our own learning.

God,
Even though it is hard to articulate,
I long to have my needs for worthiness met.
I long to know that I am heard and not useless in
*   this world.*
In those moments when I feel that my needs are
*   not met,*
I tend to withdraw and grow even quieter, and in
*   that place,*
I feel alone.

Thank you for your presence in the places of my heart
where my ineffable sorrows seem like too much.
Thank you for holding my inarticulable needs and
    giving me courage,
in grace, to speak,
one word at a time,
one moment at a time.
In you, I am humbly reminded that I am so much
    more than my ego.
I am free to let go,
and be lifted, in you.
Amen.

HOW TO GO DEEPER

A FEW YEARS AGO, I MOVED to a new city where I was instantly overwhelmed by the process of making friends and building community. Up until this point I had lived in my home state, where my community consisted of people I'd met in college or knew from church. Now, at various work functions, I was meeting other young women who wanted to get together for coffee. Not really knowing where to begin with this whole community-building thing, I just said yes to whoever asked.

About a month into this, I was exhausted. When I wasn't working, I was tucked in a coffee shop telling my life story and listening to someone else tell theirs. The women I met were kind and many of them invited me to other social gatherings around the city. I was grateful to have a long list of acquaintances, but it was a lot to keep up with. Following up with text messages and social media updates only added to the exhaustion I was beginning to experience.

So I made a spreadsheet. I made an actual spreadsheet of nearly everyone I had spent time with in the city. I created columns for names, where we met, where they were from, mutual friends, and the date we last got together.

I created this list out of des-peration as I tried to keep up with my rapidly changing social life, but it ended up being a helpful tool. It allowed me to see that even though I felt like I couldn't keep up socially, all along I had been present. All along I had managed to re-member little details about my  new acquaintances' lives, even though we had met for coffee only once. Looking at my spreadsheet, I was proud of myself. I had become so accustomed to comparing myself to how others built community that I realized I hadn't re-served any time to observe my own strengths.

From this list I was able to decide which acquaintances I wanted to go deeper with. I was able to be at peace with knowing that even though I couldn't keep up with everyone, the fact that we had been present to one another mattered.

As Fives, we are easily overwhelmed when building rela-tionships because it takes a lot of energy for us to be present with people. However, we are free to take time to reflect. We are free to go into a quiet place, seeking wisdom and discernment on how to navigate moving forward and going deeper. In grace, there is time.

Jesus often withdrew to lonely places and prayed. (Luke 5:16)

When we think of the life of Jesus, our minds may be drawn to the many portrayals of his constant and consistent connection with others. This is also true: he often withdrew. He often went away to pray. When it comes to fast-paced patterns of community and social life, we are free to take this time too.

How can you withdraw today in a mindful way?

PRACTICING
GENEROSITY

ONE OF THE WAYS I have been able to overcome the lie that I will never be prepared is by practicing generosity. The key word here is *practice* because generosity doesn't come easily to me. It's not that I'm trying to be selfish or stingy, but when it comes to my mind, I feel like I just don't have enough of it to go around. I tell myself that I must hold on to my saved time as much as I can. I must preserve my energy because it is easily depleted.

However, when I look back over my life, I find that over and over again, God has revealed something important to me. Yes, I have been uniquely gifted in being mindful of time and energy and in thinking things through, but this is also true: I can share what I've learned with others.

Productivity consultant David Allen said, "Your mind is for having ideas, not holding them." If you find it hard to get out of your head and share with others, start by writing down your ideas or capturing them on a voice recorder. These are just small steps that can create pathways for you to re-enter and engage with the world.

It's okay if you don't get it right all the time. It's okay to learn as you go. Of course, there are people who try to take advantage of others' time and energy, but this is not true of everyone. There are plenty of people who, if you spent a little more time with them than you normally would, might provide insights and support for which you are grateful, even if the conversation did require a lot of time or energy.

When it comes to practicing generosity, perfection is not the goal. What matters is taking a deep breath, remembering the ground beneath your feet, and making the brave choice to live with an open heart.

In 1 Timothy 6:18 Paul says, "Be generous and willing to share." Start with a willing mind and an open heart. Start by practicing. Observe your community and contemplate how you might get involved. In what ways can you show up? Listen to your family or the people you interact with on a daily basis. How can you be present with them in a way that doesn't rely on words? How can you show up with a mind, heart, and body that is ready to serve?

It will take great strength to do this, but the beautiful thing is this: you are free to practice. You are free to trust that you will be provided with the right amount of time and energy to give to others.

How can you practice generosity today?

PRACTICING PATIENCE: AN INVITATION

WHATEVER QUESTIONS YOU are living with right now, do not take away from what is already true: even here, there is more to you. Even here, you are free to feel the soil beneath your feet and fully engage in life. As a Five, you are naturally open minded and curious, and this is also true: you are naturally equipped to just be, right here in the waiting.

Have patience. Have patience for all you have yet to learn and all that has yet to be revealed to you. Practice your patience by being present right here in this moment, knowing it will never be here again. Gwendolyn Brooks writes:

Exhaust the little moment. Soon it dies.
And be it gash or gold it will not come
Again in this identical disguise.

You are becoming who you were meant to be even in the silence while you wait for God to speak. The earth is still filled with life. The birds still migrate south. The flowers still spring up from the ground. All around is life that you may not be able to see when you rush from one thought to the next.

Slow down. Be curious about what could be and also curious about what God is nudging you to attend to in this moment. Time is limited, but there is still time for you to slow down and pay attention to what is flourishing within you.

While you have this morning, this afternoon, or this evening, trust that you do not have to know what's to come or what lurks in the shadows of the future. Trust that this very moment matters in a million subtle ways, and you are free to find joy where you are. Whatever is happening right here, no matter how small, is a reminder that amid all that is happening and all that could go wrong, grace will find you. You are a part of something greater than you, no matter who made you feel small. Look closely at the length of this morning, this afternoon. Breathe deep and be reminded: You are part of this life. You have not been left out just because you don't know what the future looks like. You are not worth any less as you wait to see what waits on the other end of your questions.

> Wait for the LORD;
> be strong and take heart
> and wait for the LORD. (Psalm 27:14)

> *God,*
> *Give me strength today to practice patience.*

Even when things don't go according to plan,
and even when my train of thought is interrupted,
may I continue to breathe deep and trust that
I have not missed out on what was meant for me.
You have so much more for me to see,
even if it looks different from what I expected.
I am guided. I am directed.
Teach me to stay curious and openhearted
and wait patiently for you.
Amen.

FREIGHT TRAINS

WHEN I WAS A KID, at least once or twice a month my family would be late for Wednesday night church because of a freight train. There was only one way to get from our house to the church, and that road crossed a highly trafficked train track.

There was no alternate route, so there was nothing to do but wait. Sometimes we would wait there for twenty minutes (at least that's how it seemed in my brain at the time). With nothing else to do but sit in the back seat and stare out the window, I grew accustomed to noticing each train car as it went by.

I was mesmerized by the variety in color and also the big letters and numbers painted boldly on the sides. To me these train cars were a great mystery. What items did they hold? I would imagine each one filled with treasures—one was carrying boxes of books, the next Cabbage Patch Kids dolls, the next Hot Wheels racetracks . . . I would go on and on until I eventually ran out of ideas.

I have always had a tendency to divide things into categories. This has proven to be a helpful trait when I'm working on a project or trying to prioritize a set of tasks. However, it is less helpful in other ways.

When I was a kid sitting in the back seat of my parents' car, one thing I didn't pay attention to was the freight train as a whole. I loved to focus on the individual cars and

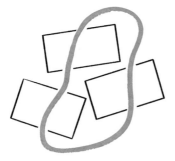 imagine all they contained, but the fact that all these different things were traveling together on one train was a wonder all on its own.

Sometimes, as a Five, I find it hard to zoom out and look at the whole thing. Dividing things into categories comes naturally to me. But in Christ, I find that something beautiful happens when those segments are brought back together. Suddenly I am able to experience love that "surpasses knowledge." By letting the cars all run together, I make room for wholeness in my life.

How have you compartmentalized your life? Are there ways you could zoom out and look at the whole?

FRIEND GROUPS

UNTIL I DISCOVERED THE ENNEAGRAM, I hadn't realized that my tendency to compartmentalize meant I had been segmenting my friend groups. There were my college friends, church friends, musician friends, and family friends, and in my mind those groups did not overlap.

For this reason I never wanted to have birthday parties, because the idea of all of these different people in a room together brought me great anxiety. How on earth would they connect? What would they even talk about? The idea left me bewildered for years, and I always shied away from the idea of a party—until my most recent birthday, when I decided to give it a try.

I stressed about the party literally until the first guest arrived. My heart pounded out of my chest as friends and family from different backgrounds who didn't know each other gathered in the room.

And just like that, I couldn't believe what was happening —everything was fine. People mingled and blended and many even walked away with new friends. I didn't understand how it happened, but perhaps that was the lesson. I didn't have to understand how. I could trust that it all came together without me.

> I pray that you . . . grasp how wide and long and high and deep is the love of Christ, and . . . know this love that surpasses knowledge—that you may be filled to the measure of all the fullness of God. (Ephesians 3:17-19)

Do you keep your friend groups separate? Where is there room to soften these boundaries? What do you think would happen if you hosted an event where several of these groups were invited to mingle and merge?

ONE FEELING
AT A TIME

FROM A DISTANCE, it might seem that Fives don't really feel their feelings. Because we Fives have a hard time identifying our emotions in the moment, we may come across as uninvolved or disconnected in some way—often without even realizing it.

As a Five, I am on a journey of learning to work through this by focusing on one feeling at a time. I am learning that I don't have to figure out how to feel everything at once, even if others seem much more in tune with what they're feeling. Yes, I am aware that I need to grow as a Five, but I don't have to try to cover all the ground in the landscape right away. I can choose to start slow. I can choose to begin with the feelings I can identify first.

One thing that has helped me articulate my emotions is the Feelings Inventory offered by the Center for Nonviolent Communication (see cnvc.org/training/resource/feelings-inventory).

I'll never forget the day my therapist handed this list to me a few years ago. As I read through it, my shoulders loosened and I felt myself exhale. I was reminded that navigating through feelings isn't as simple as saying I was "happy," "sad," or "upset." There are many words for expressing different emotional states.

"I feel elated."

"I feel relaxed."

"I feel sleepy."

"I feel nostalgic."

I walked out of my therapy session excited about this newfound territory to explore. And this time it wasn't a book to read. It wasn't a Wikipedia rabbit hole to tumble down. This time it was using language—something I dearly loved—to express what I was feeling outside my head and in the real world.

A heart at peace gives life to the body. (Proverbs 14:30)

As you read this, I hope you can take a deep breath. I hope you can trust that even though the landscape of emotion may be overwhelming, there are places you can start. Even if the only words you have right now are, "I don't know what I'm feeling," that's still a beginning. That's still one step on the journey of opening up and being present to what God might reveal to you right here where you are.

You are free to begin the journey of experiencing the full range of your emotions, even if you start by identifying one feeling at a time.

> *God,*
> *I come to you today,*
> *taking one breath at a time.*
> *There is no need to rush*
> *in your Presence.*
> *As I learn to articulate what I am feeling,*
> *I will also learn that in grace,*
> *it is okay to pace myself.*
> *It is okay if this takes time.*
> *You are with me every step of this journey.*
> *May my soul remain unhurried*
> *in your Love.*
> *Amen.*

SHARING OUR
KNOWLEDGE

FIVES LOVE ACQUIRING KNOWLEDGE, but at times it's hard for us to share our knowledge with others. Even when we get past the feeling of being unprepared to share, we still confront the reality that others may not be interested in the same topics or share the same ideas. We may loan books to friends who never let us know if they read them or not. We may be asked to help solve a problem, and once the problem is solved, find that no one seems to care about it anymore.

In these moments we may start to feel lonely or useless. We may start to wonder, *What's the point of sharing what we're learning if no one wants to listen?*

May we never give up on connection because of those who do not respond the way we think they will. When we share, may we do it from a place much deeper than wanting others to be "in the know." May we share because we want to join in on the bigger conversation and be a part of the greater story, God's story.

Sometimes our words will be heard, and other times our presence will be felt. And that is more than enough. We do not have to bring the solution in order to have value.

Sometimes, when we don't get the response we were hoping for, we can feel that we are not needed. In those moments, let's remember this: acts of love are never useless. Even when they are not reciprocated in the way we hope they will be. When we choose to share for love, it matters. We are still sowing seeds for what is to come.

More than desiring to be heard, let us identify ways we can live the things we have studied. How can we apply our research and knowledge to real-life scenarios? If we feel a desire to share (or at least to challenge ourselves to share), what settings will allow us to be teachers?

My people, hear my teaching;
    listen to the words of my mouth.
I will open my mouth with a parable;
    I will utter hidden things, things from of old—
things we have heard and known,
    things our ancestors have told us.
We will not hide them from their descendants;
    we will tell the next generation

the praiseworthy deeds of the LORD,
> his power, and the wonders he has done.
>> (Psalm 78:1-4)

You may not be able to be a teacher in every setting, but there are places in this world and in your very community that are looking for teachers. There might be a student out there right now searching the internet for an answer you can help her with. Don't be discouraged. There is room for you to share, wholeheartedly.

God,
I give thanks to you for being my Teacher.
Thank you for the wisdom you have woven
throughout my life.
Give me strength to be an example of Christ-Love,
guided by your Spirit
anytime I have the opportunity to share wisdom or
knowledge with others.
May you help me grow in my awareness of my
own limitations
and keep a humble heart.
May I listen more than I rely on speaking.
May I trust more than I rely on thinking.
Help me to remember the fullness and wonder of all
you are
beyond my deepest understandings.
Amen.

What happens when you begin to share your knowledge and it's not received in the way you expected?

COURAGE AND GRACE: AN INVITATION

THIS IS COURAGE: coming alive in new unknowns even though you have no idea what lies before you. It is the ability to trust that even though you do not know all the details of the forest you travel through, you are still traveling, and that's what matters. You are learning to see that even when you feel limited on resources, there is grace.

Grace to notice the song of the birds and the sweet vanilla scent of the ponderosa pines gently blowing in the air. Grace that allows you to see the richness of life, even when your mind races with uncertainty. Even then, you are still awake. As fallen twigs snap beneath your feet and you place your hand on the century-old bark of trees, let it be in the wilderness that you are reminded of the wholeness of it all. God is here, in all things great and small.

I am making a way in the wilderness. (Isaiah 43:19)

Now that you know this, you do not have to go to sleep to yourself. Now that you are noticing more of what's around you, you are starting to see that all along, you could only plan so much, and that's okay. Continue to take this path through the wild day by day, bravely moving forward even as you wait for your energy to be restored.

You are not wasting time. This forest is filled with endless unknowns, but endless light will guide you and remind you that even here, you are not alone. There is more to experience, far beyond what your mind first notices. Far beyond what your eyes can see. Alberto Ríos writes:

> By only looking without listening, you will not hear
> the trees.
> You will see only hard stone and flattened landscape,
> But if you're quiet, you will hear it.

Whenever you start to feel restless, like you're going in circles and there's no way out, remember how long the forest took to grow into what it is today. Listen. Hear the sound of the leaves and let them remind you of their aliveness. Here there is peace. It takes courage to feel this. Trust that in grace, you are capable.

> **Where have you been courageous in the wilderness this week? As you reflect on this, how do you feel in your heart? How do you feel in your body?**

IT'S TIME TO EAT

PAYING ATTENTION TO and taking care of our bodies is an essential part of being human. However, in my Fiveness, I tend to overthink even this. My inner dialogue sometimes looks like this: *Okay, I've been at my desk for hours. I need to do something. I know, I'll take a walk. Eh, maybe not, because it probably won't be that peaceful considering it's already the afternoon and everyone else is out. Maybe I'll just clean up the kitchen. But honestly—that could wait till later. I'll go sit on the deck for a bit—or maybe not; I'll just start worrying about the dead plants I need to dispose of. All right, I'll just finish working through this next chapter, and then I'll be finished for the day.*

Just like that, I've talked myself out of the possibility of getting up and getting into my body.

When I think about what I need to do to "get into my body," the first thing that comes to mind is eating a meal. I wish I had a more intellectual inclination, but the reality is, I need my basic needs met like everyone else. Sometimes I feel a little antsy and don't know why. Reading a favorite poem or writing in my journal might calm me down, but more often than not, I look at the clock and realize I just worked my way through lunch. The answer is right there in my belly. I need to eat.

As Fives we can most certainly learn to pay attention and notice our bodies when we go for the walk, join that gym class, or clean out the garage over the weekend. However, we also learn to do this by taking time to eat. By truly tasting the seasonings and the mix of textures. By noticing how our bodies feel when we eat certain foods.

This practical gesture is a part of accepting who we are. There will be moments for grand gestures, but there will also be moments to sit by the window with a sandwich or a bowl of soup, and that matters for our bodies too. Let's take a deep breath now. Sometimes "getting into our bodies" is really that simple. What a gift.

> Eat honey, my son, for it is good;
>> honey from the comb is sweet to your taste.
>>> (Proverbs 24:13)

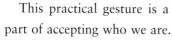

Eat your next meal mindfully. Chew slowly. Think about who prepared the food. What tastes do you pay the most attention to? How does your body feel after the meal?

PRACTICE GENTLENESS

ONE OF MY MOST EMBARRASSING moments happened in a high school debate class. The classroom was split into two teams, and I was on the team arguing in favor of the topic. I spent days preparing for the debate, determined that my team would win.

Unfortunately, when the day of the debate came, the other team had managed to prepare a bit more in its defense. My team lost, but I couldn't accept defeat. I had done the research. I knew I was right. The topic was something I was incredibly passionate about (the future of digital music distribution), and I was certain I had the facts on my side. I kept going, trying to prove my point over and over.

Meanwhile, my teammates had already waved their white flags and headed back to their seats. But I didn't notice. It wasn't until our teacher whispered in the calmest voice, "Okay, Morgan, that's enough now."

Her words brought me out of my head and back to the room, and I looked around. All of my classmates were staring at me, and the look in their eyes wasn't as kind as our teacher's. To me, their collective glare said, "Are you done now, Morgan? Can you cool it?"

I hung my head low as I walked back to my seat. I was humiliated. I couldn't find the words to speak or the strength to make eye contact for the rest of the day.

In that moment I had lacked all gentleness. I had put all my trust in my hard shell of knowledge, thinking it would save the day. I had tricked myself into thinking that if I just kept creating scenario after scenario, eventually others would get my point.

But in that moment, my teacher's gentleness showed me that it was not about being right. In that moment, quite practically, it was about finishing the assignment and going home for the day.

As Fives, we sometimes think we are getting to the point. Debating feels like uncovering the truth, and it's just a matter of time before everyone else sees it. But in reality, even when we have a legitimate point, sometimes dinner is ready. Sometimes class is over. Sometimes the conversation has simply carried on too long. It's time to back away, with gentleness.

A gentle answer turns away wrath,
but a harsh word stirs up anger. (Proverbs 15:1)

When we are able to back away with gentleness, we see that we are capable of letting go. We see that even when the conversation has moved on to something else, we still belong. The time we shared together was meaningful even if we didn't get to say everything we wanted to say. We can still find peace. We can still be gentle with ourselves and others.

When was the last time you were angry? Reflect on that moment. How can you practice gentleness the next time you feel anger rising?

RECEIVE THE LIGHT

AS FIVES, WE MAY UNDERSTAND intellectually that we have physical needs—vitamin D, food, water, oxygen—but other needs can be harder to express. We struggle to let others know what we need because it feels like we are inviting an invasion of privacy. To let them into our space means we have to face not only our own emotions but theirs too.

As a Five who is still learning to express my needs, I have found that simply communicating this fact has been incredibly freeing. I am free to actually say, "I am still learning to express my needs."

Instead of changing the conversation or ignoring my needs altogether, I am slowly learning to let my loved ones know that I am still figuring out how to communicate my needs. I have found this helpful whether someone asks for my help or I have identified an area where I need support.

Another thing I am learning over and over again is the grace-filled, liberating opportunity to take baby steps. It may seem like a huge task to ask someone for emotional support, but what if we just asked our spouse to help us create a grocery list? What if we asked a friend to help us find something to wear to an event?

Even when we feel like we don't need help and we could technically do it on our own, this is a chance to practice opening up, which will gradually beam into other areas of our lives.

As the leaves on the trees need the sun, so do we. We must allow ourselves to be seen by others. We must learn to practice courage by talking about our needs out loud. This can be a challenge for Fives such as myself who may not want to have a lot of attention on them. We may feel as though our needs are not important or we are inconveniencing others by expressing them. However, even though it may not feel like in the moment, when we say, "I need some time alone," we are taking a brave step. We are acknowledging that we have a need that needs to be met, and we are allowed to make that known. In that moment, we are allowing ourselves to be seen by others, whether or not they respond with grace and compassion. The first step is speaking up and coming out of hiding.

When someone is responding to your need, you may feel like the blinds have been opened and afternoon sun is beaming down on you a little too strongly. The heat of the light may feel overwhelming at first, and at the same time, your body needs sunlight. You have needs that need to be met and they cannot be met if you are hiding in the shadows, inside.

When we express our needs to others, we are letting light in. We are letting the attention be on ourselves for a moment in a way that allows others to help and support us. It takes great vulnerability to let ourselves be seen in this way because we don't know how people will respond. If you've been lurking in the shadows of not expressing your needs, you might feel overwhelmed by the sudden light of a loved one or a friend knowing intimate details about you. And at the same time, you need light. Even if you have to inch your way there, welcoming light in small doses, it's necessary for your growth.

Breathe deep and open yourself up to receive the light of human connection. Let today be when you allow yourself to practice courage by allowing yourself to be seen by others.

Read the following verse and then pray and contemplate:

Remain in me, as I also remain in you. No branch can bear fruit by itself; it must remain in the vine. Neither can you bear fruit unless you remain in me. (John 15:4)

AN INWARD
OBSERVATION

IN *THE SPIRITUAL DIMENSION OF THE ENNEAGRAM,* Sandra
Maitri writes, "In order to let go of needing foreknowledge
about her inner process . . . a Five will have to confront the
fear that drives this need, the fear of experiencing herself
exactly as she is."

Reading these words, I am reminded to be still with an
unhurried mind. I am reminded that beneath my tendency
to fill the space in my head with ideas and concepts is a fear
I must work through.

I must work through the fear of being helpless.

I must work through the belief that I don't have enough
to cope with life.

I must trust that I am more prepared than I think.

In the same way we Fives have been equipped to be observers and see things objectively, as they are, we have also
been equipped to see ourselves as we are. As Fives, we are

able to learn a great deal about others by listening to them, so imagine what would happen if you started listening to yourself. Imagine what you might discover by spending fifteen minutes in solitude and silence today. Even if you walk away without new thoughts or ideas, you will walk away knowing you were still connected to this life. You will find that God speaks not only in silence and stillness, but also through it.

The LORD will fight for you; you need only to be still. (Exodus 14:14)

Dare to take the journey within. Dare to sit with what you're feeling in your body and the emotions you're able

to identify, no matter how vague they may be. It's worth it. You're worth it.

There is no need to be afraid of silence. For even there you are loved. The inner landscape is much more than the desert it often feels like. There are mountains, rivers, valleys, sun, and stars that fill the sky. How great thou art. What a miracle you are, even when you can't intellectualize it. Be still in the silence. Trust that you are worthy of the same observation and attention you give to many other things.

May you look at the trees outside your window a little longer today and listen to the lyrics of the song you love a bit more closely. Pay attention to the distinct taste of the natural sugar in the fruit you just bit into. Experience what is valuable in life as it is. And perhaps, from there, you can begin to see that you too are valuable as you are. Perhaps you don't have to learn anything else about yourself before you choose to say, "I am whole."

God,
Today I am slowing down long enough
to simply be in awe of your Creation.
I am noticing what is beautiful, knowing I am free
    to simply notice.
I am free to simply be.
I do not have to try to intellectualize.
Thank you for giving me this moment, just to be
    here, in the stillness.
Thank you for generously reminding me, right here,
    in awe of your Creation,
that I am worthy of Divine Love and Belonging,
    right here, as I am.
Amen.

Where (or with whom) do you feel loved as you are? Write about what that feels like. If nothing comes to mind, describe what you desire to feel when it comes to love.

THERE IS A PLACE FOR YOU: AN INVITATION

TAKE HEART AND BREATHE THIS IN: you do not have to grow where everyone else grows in order to have a meaningful life. Some of the most beautiful things grow in seemingly unlikely places. Plants do not grow only in the fresh soil of rolling green fields that receive the right amount of sunshine and rain. They do not grow only in well-lit spots that make up perfectly landscaped beds. They also grow underwater, in the dark, in the winter, in the desert. They grow in the places most would never think to look.

May you never compare yourself to those who grow in more lively environments. May you trust that your contribution matters, even if it seems subtle. As a Five, you may look at what you're working on as inferior because the impact isn't as instantaneous as someone else's project. You might see others taking action out in public and begin to question the work you're doing behind the scenes. You might think less of the research you've put in because you aren't as noisy as others. Perhaps you gave a lot of time and energy to a presentation but your colleague's report made everyone laugh and thus was the one everyone remembered.

Even then, you are not worth any less. Like a coral reef that provides shelter and food for thousands of fish under the sea, your presence matters in places unlikely to be noticed. The coral reef protects coastlines and communities, offering protection from storms and erosion. Indigenous people around the world rely on coral reefs for their basic needs. And yet the reef never speaks. We never hear her voice. She never rises up out of the ocean. And yet she is worthy of care. She has a purpose that goes beyond what most people notice.

There are many hidden, quiet places in nature that are much more significant than we may initially notice. All around us and below us, God has filled the earth with life. It comes in the forms of birds singing high in the trees or cheetahs tracking across the Serengeti. Life is present and filled with purpose far beyond what we can see.

God saw all that he had made, and it was very good. (Genesis 1:31)

Take heart and breathe this in: no matter how many times you have compared yourself to others or felt overlooked, there is a place for you in this world and in your community, no matter how different you feel.

God,
I am so grateful that you are all-knowing.
I am grateful that you see beyond what most eyes see,
from particles of dust floating between the half-
*   opened miniblinds to*
the often overlooked and forgotten coral reef.
Thank you for reminding me that even when I am
*   not seen by others,*
I am seen by you.
Always.
Amen.

KEEP SOWING SEEDS

IT'S OKAY IF CHANGE HAPPENS SLOWLY. Like a garden cultivated on the rooftop of a sprawling city, what matters is the first seed that's sown. What matters is the first person who tells a neighbor to come and plant something of their own. What matters is the daily choice to care for these seeds, over and over, day after day, even when no one else feels like it, even when others move on to other things.

As Fives, when we are in a healthy place, we "are sensitive to our environments and perceive subtle change," write Don Richard Riso and Russ Hudson in *The Wisdom of the Enneagram*. When we choose to live mindfully, focusing on one thing at a time, we are able to focus with a great sense of patience.

Think of the projects you've started and the curiosities

you've pursued. You haven't looked for easy answers and you've allowed yourself to be comfortable with the process. Even when you haven't gotten the results you were looking for, the time and energy you invested has helped you grow in your expertise.

Over and over, when you have sat down with your books, at your computer, or in your garden, you have been faithfully sowing seeds. Even though you didn't know what the *Farmers' Almanac* would reveal and how the weather would change, you showed up to the page, the Word document, or the flowerpot anyway. Keep doing this. All it takes is one seed.

Who dares despise the day of small things?
(Zechariah 4:10)

Never forget the small beginnings. Never forget that God uses them. Let the seemingly insignificant moments teach you. Let an overheard joke bring joy to your soul. Keep your heart open. Keep going back to the garden. Water your plants daily, even if you don't know when, where, or how they'll grow.

Keep sowing seeds of what is good and true, knowing that the things you do quietly and slowly speak volumes about your character and faithfulness.

God,
Thank you for the gift of small beginnings.
Thank you for making space for mustard
   seed–like faith.

*Thank you for loving me in such a way that I know
   I am free
to take the little energy I have and still sow seeds.
Others may look at what I'm working on and not be
   able to see the picture.
In fact, if I truly slow down and think about it, I
   can't see the whole picture either.
But here's where I find peace: I find peace in
   knowing, in your omnipresence,
that you see it all.
You see what the seed can be before it is even sown.
You see the fullness of the soil even before the
   flowers grow.
Thank you for your divine attention
to even the smallest things.
Amen.*

YOU ARE MORE PREPARED THAN YOU THINK

WHILE PREPARING TO WRITE today's reading, I combed through a box of old journals from my college years. I found this entry from twelve years ago, right before I began my sophomore year:

July 12, 2008
Endlessness Without Emptiness

There's a part of me that wants to be remembered, and at the same time, there's something intriguing to me about this endless feeling of not knowing what to expect in the next thirty years, thirty days, or thirty seconds. It's a contradiction, a paradox, something I can't seem to classify, but through all of this, I am learning the simple art of satisfaction. I am finding that it is achievable not through people or earthly securities, but through God-given peace that I might just have to fight every day to hold onto, and to me, that is all that matters . . . and the only way I can embrace the endlessness without sinking down into emptiness.

I wrote this entry as I was preparing to transfer to a new school. Back then I struggled making friends, and I was wondering if my classmates and dormmates would even remember me as I prepared to move away. Even though I was usually content being alone, I still wanted to belong. I didn't mind waiting, but I didn't want to feel empty.

I knew nothing of the Enneagram at that time, but in those words I can see a young woman who was desperate to find peace for her uncertainty. I can see that she hadn't figured it out and was trying to find the right words for what she was thinking. I can also see that she was trying. I can see that even though her mind was filled with questions, they were not too confusing or strange to be held in the arms of grace.

She couldn't see it then, but amid her worries about the future, God was already strengthening her. She was more equipped for the next chapter than she realized.

May this be the chapter in your story where you look back and realize you were more prepared than you thought you were. You were not useless, even when your inner thoughts told you otherwise. You had the ability to feel your emotions and be present to your body, even though there were many moments when all you wanted to do was withdraw.

Even then, you chose to live courageously. You did not draw conclusions. You kept an open mind and also a heart that was open to the hope of what could be, even when you faced uncertainty.

There is always room for growth, but this is also true: you have already come so far. You live in a fast-paced, busy world that doesn't seem to leave a lot of room for Fives to take their time to process. And yet here you are, every day, making the most of where you are.

I hope you continue to make room for growth in this chapter of your story, and I hope you also recognize all the ways you have already grown. No matter what unknown lies ahead, you are already making it through. God is still strengthening you and preparing the way. There is no need to hide any longer. There is no need to be afraid.

I can do all this through him who gives me strength. Yet it was good of you to share in my troubles. (Philippians 4:13-14)

As a Five, you may encounter a feeling of emptiness on the journey. You may desire to let others in but struggle to figure out where to begin. But this is also true: you were never meant to travel alone. We have one another. Not only do we have other Fives, but we also have friend groups, families, and communities that we are worthy of being a part of, right here, right now.

Go back through an old journal entry (even if it's from just a few weeks ago). Write a new journal entry as an ode to how far you have come.

ENNEAGRAM
DAILY REFLECTIONS

SUZANNE STABILE,
SERIES EDITOR

Forty Days on Being a One
Juanita Rasmus

Forty Days on Being a Two
Hunter Mobley

Forty Days on Being a Three
Sean Palmer

Forty Days on Being a Four
Christine Yi Suh

Forty Days on Being a Five
Morgan Harper Nichols

Forty Days on Being a Six
Tara Beth Leach

Forty Days on Being a Seven
Gideon Yee Shun Tsang

Forty Days on Being an Eight
Sandra Maria Van Opstal—Fall 2021

Forty Days on Being a Nine
Marlena Graves